VIDEO BOOK

MATT SCHOFIELD
BLUES GUITAR ARTISTRY
TASTE, TONE & TECHNIQUE

To access video visit:
www.halleonard.com/mylibrary

Enter Code
1520-6526-9650-6720

ISBN 978-1-5400-5468-5

HAL•LEONARD®

Visit Hal Leonard Online at
www.halleonard.com

Contact us:
Hal Leonard
7777 West Bluemound Road
Milwaukee, WI 53213
Email: info@halleonard.com

In Europe, contact:
Hal Leonard Europe Limited
42 Wigmore Street
Marylebone, London, W1U 2RN
Email: info@halleonardeurope.com

In Australia, contact:
Hal Leonard Australia Pty. Ltd.
4 Lentara Court
Cheltenham, Victoria, 3192 Australia
Email: info@halleonard.com.au

Introduction

Welcome to *Blues Guitar Artistry: Taste, Tone & Technique*. This book/online video package is a masterclass in playing blues guitar taught by British Blues Guitar Hall of Fame artist, Matt Schofield. In this 70+ minute video, Matt presents the various techniques he uses to express himself and connect more deeply with his listeners. His mission is to help you develop your individual style and tone—your unique voice.

Tone is not something you buy. Sure, the instruments, amplifiers, and effects you choose are all part of the equation, but your individual tone lies in your hands—and how you use them! Matt demonstrates how he holds the pick, and offers his insight into how the tonal palate changes depending on where and how the strings are struck; both are fundamental ways to add emotion to your playing. Applying his techniques to bends, slides, and vibratos will help bring a rich vocal quality to your sound.

While we're on the topic of bends, Matt demonstrates how to add tension and release using various degrees of string bends. He also teaches a series of chord inversions up and down the fretboard, and explains how to incorporate double stops and triads into your solos. Of course, scale patterns are important too, but Matt goes beyond the standard pentatonic scales, adding color with the 6th, 9th, and 13th scale degrees. And let's not forget rhythm; you can get a lot of mileage from just a few notes simply by changing your rhythmic phrasing.

You'll see all of these techniques in action as he leads his band through various types of grooves and blues progressions. The examples—presented in rhythm tab, chord grids, and fretboard diagrams—will help you follow along with the video to see how note choices, bends, pick attack, and phrasing can open your music up to a more colorful and expressive dimension.

Synthesizing Your Influences

Example 1
Key of C
(0:39)

*T = Thumb on 6th string.

Example 2
(4:14)

*T=Thumb on 6th string.

Example 3
(6:39)

Slow

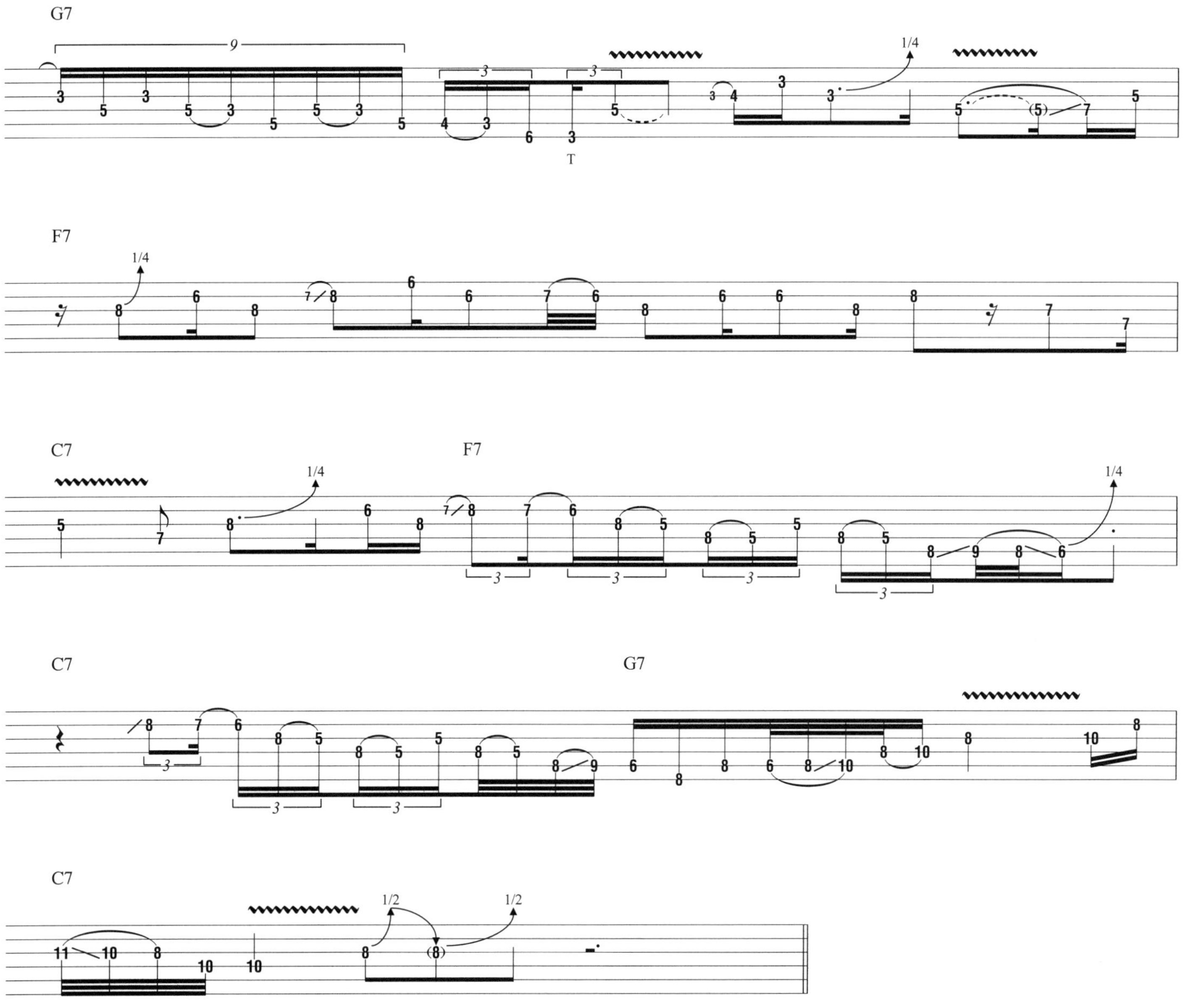
G7
F7
C7
F7
C7
G7
C7

Tone, Production and Technique

Example 4
Key of A
(1:43)

Example 5
(2:44)

Bm7

E7

A7

C7

B7

B♭7

Example 6: Dynamics of pick attack
Key of Am
(7:17)

Freely

N.C.(Am)

T
A
B

4/4

*T=Thumb on 6th string.

*T=Thumb on 6th string.

let ring - - - - - - - - -

Example 7: Pick rakes and tremolo
Key of Am
(7:55)

*T=Thumb on 6th string.

Example 8: Varying pick position along strings
Key of Cm
(8:30)

Pick near bridge

**T=Thumb on 6th string.

*T=Thumb on 6th string.

Example 9: Piano-style plucking
Key of A
(9:19)

Example 10: Fingerstyle "rolls"
Key of A
(9:30)

Example 11: Hybrid picking
Key of A
(9:45)

Example 12: Hybrid picking single notes
Key of Am
(10:22)

w/ pick & fingers

Example 13: Jam
Key of C
(10:41)

*Chord symbols reflect basic harmony.   w/ pick & fingers

*T=Thumb on 6th string.

Example 14: Vibrato
Key of A
(13:58)

Moderately fast (♩♪ = ♪♪)

*Played as even eighth notes.

Example 15: Palm muting
Key of Am
(15:27)

Freely

*T=Thumb on 6th string.

Example 16: Right-hand muting
Key of Am
(15:38)

Freely

N.C.(Am)

*T=Thumb on 6th string.

Example 17: Left-hand muting
Key of Am
(15:56)

Freely

N.C.(Am)

**T=Thumb on 6th string.

Example 18: Muted rakes
Key of A
(16:37)

Freely

N.C.(A5)

Example 19: Thumb fretting
Key of A
(17:02)

Freely

N.C.(A5)

*T=Thumb on 6th string.

Example 20: Jam
Key of C
(17:22)

Slow

N.C.

C7

*Played behind the beat.

*T

*T=Thumb on 6th string.

Extended Chord Voicings
and Blues Harmony

Example 21: A7 chord voicings
(0:26)

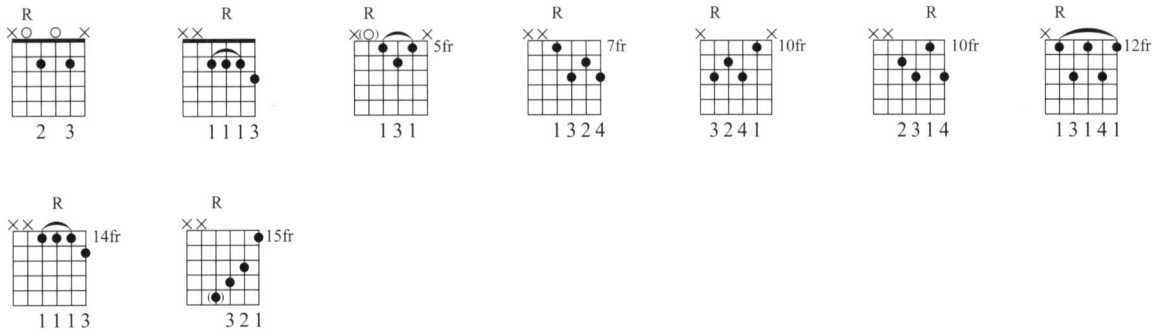

Example 22: A9 and A9♭5
(1:30)

A9   A9♭5

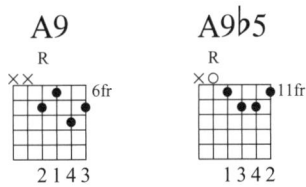

Example 23: Weaving between chords and single-note lines

Key of A

(2:46)

Moderately (♫ = ♩♪)

*T=Thumb on 5th & 6th strings.

let ring - - - ┤

*Pick w/ middle finger of picking hand.

**T
w/ fingers

**T=Thumb on 6th string.

Example 24: Comping over blues in A
Key of A
(3:58)

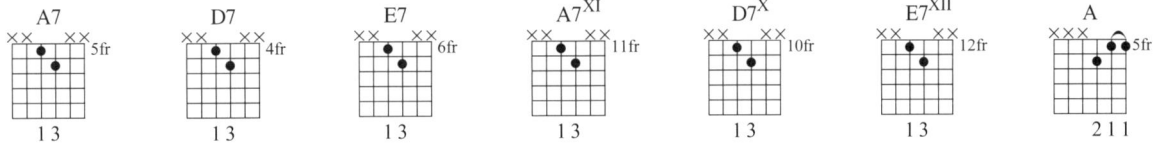

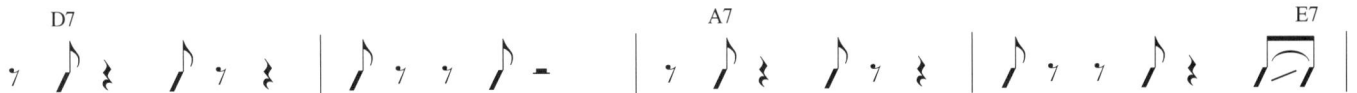

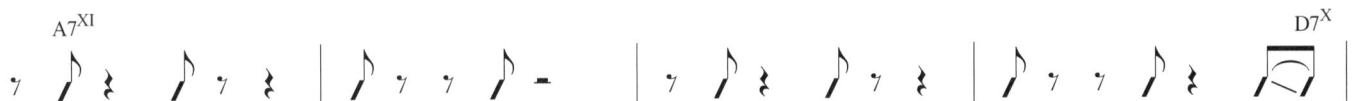

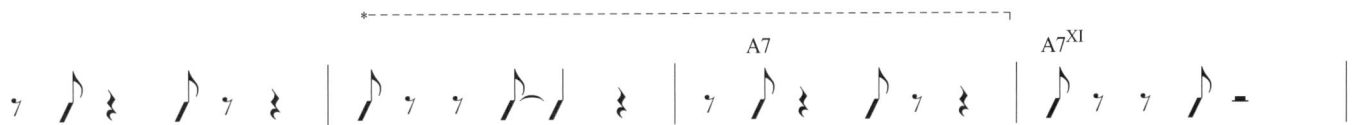

*See fill box below for notes as played.

Example 25: Extended chords
(6:13)

Example 26: Uptown chord jam
Key of A
(7:11)

Example 27: Leading tones and I-VI-ii-V
Key of A
(10:02)

Rhythm, Groove, and Timing

Example 28: "Locking in" sample jam

Key of Dm

(3:15)

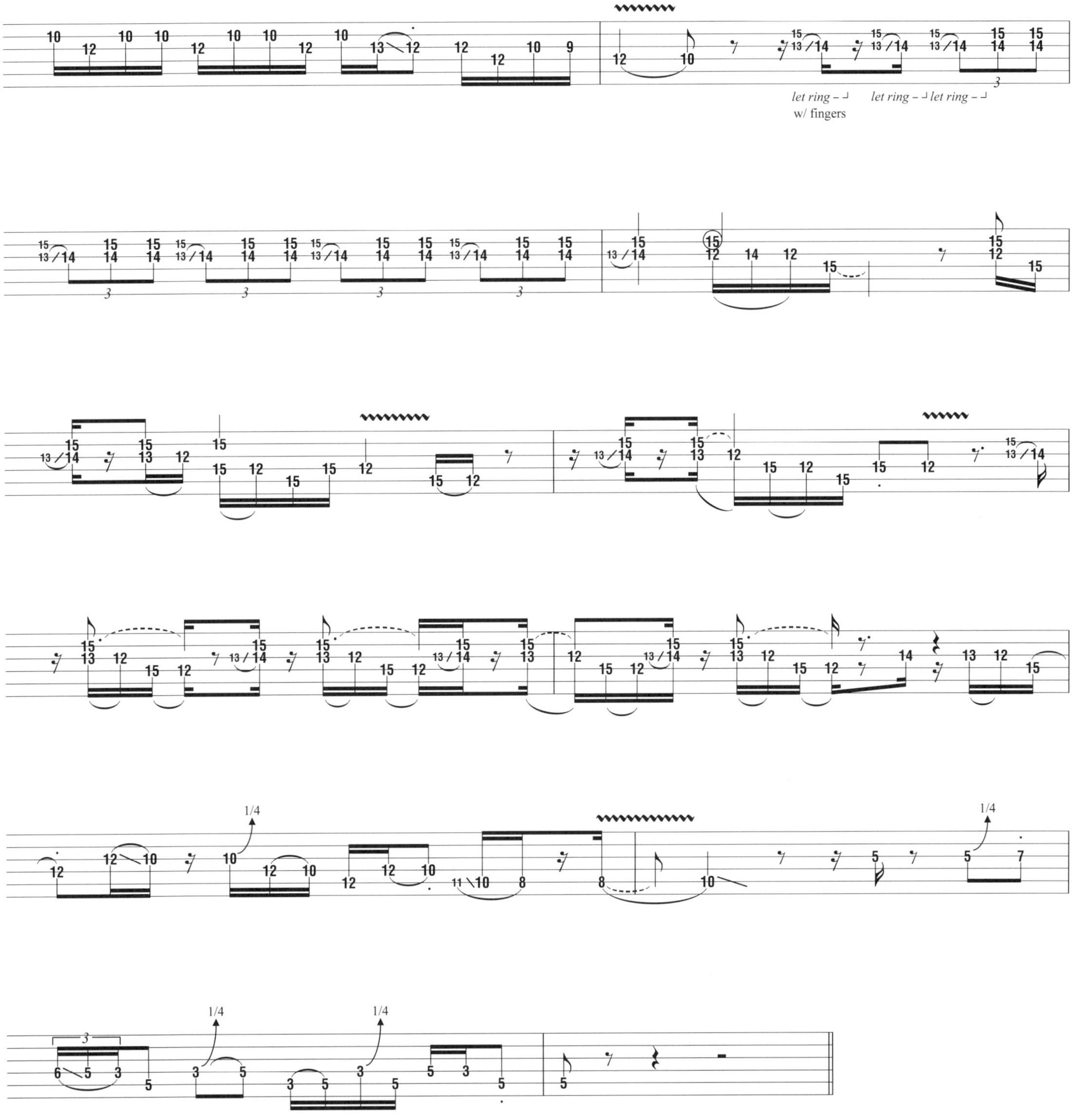
let ring
w/ fingers
let ring
let ring
1/4
1/4
1/4
1/4

Example 29: Rhythmic variation
Key of C
(6:14)

*Played behind the beat.

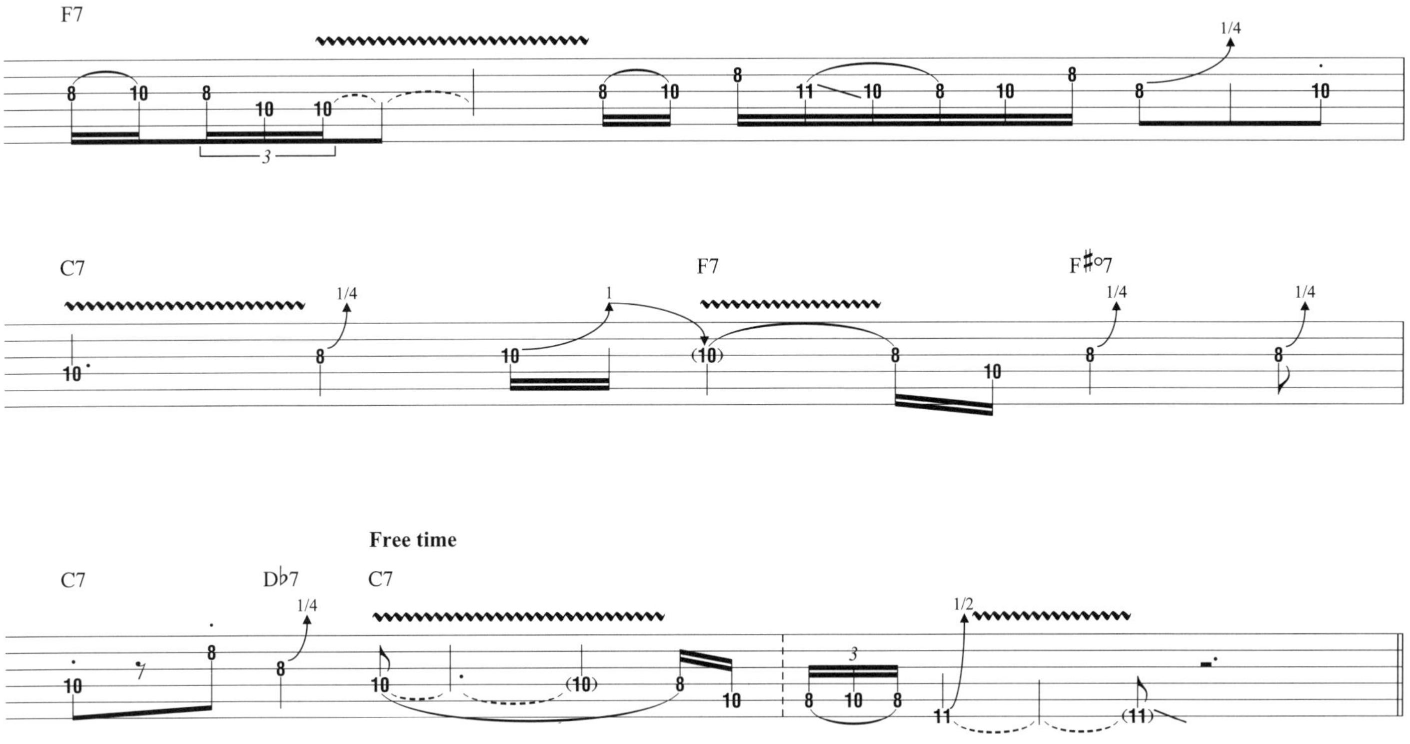
F7
C7
F7
F♯°7
C7
D♭7
Free time
C7

Fitting Your Solos to the Songs

Example 30: Scales used in blues
(0:54)

Major Pentatonic

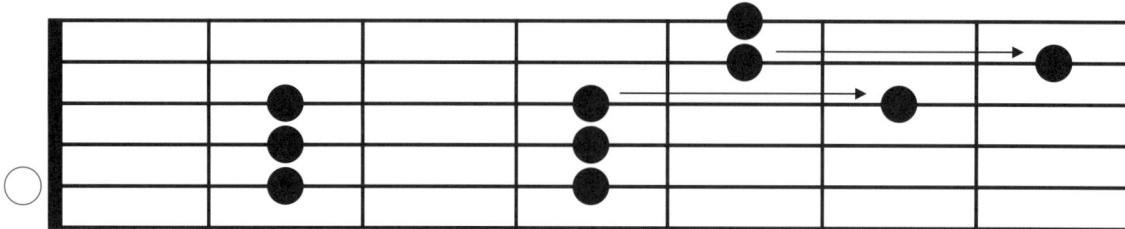

Minor Pentatonic
5fr

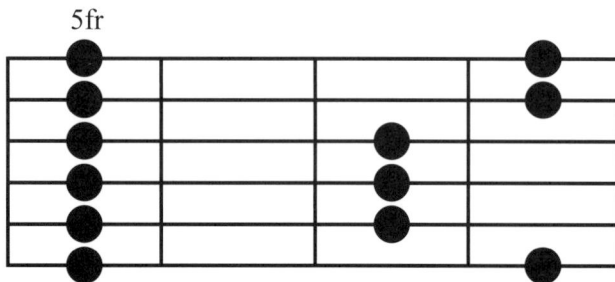

Blues Scale
5fr

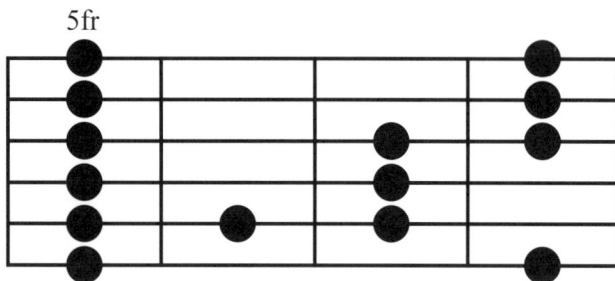

Mixolydian
4fr

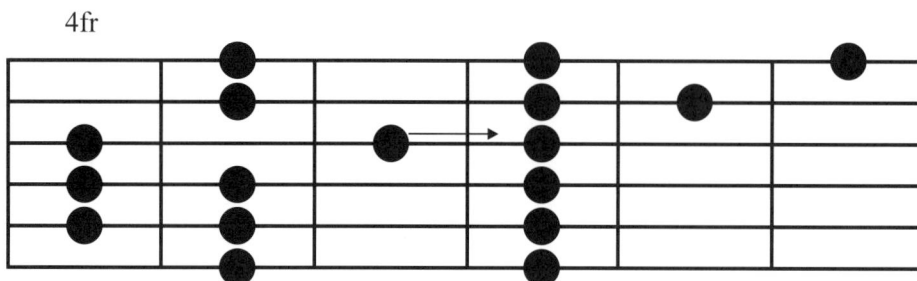

Example 31: Scales demo jam

Key of B♭

(1:56)

Moderately slow ($\sqrt{}$ = $\sqrt{}$)

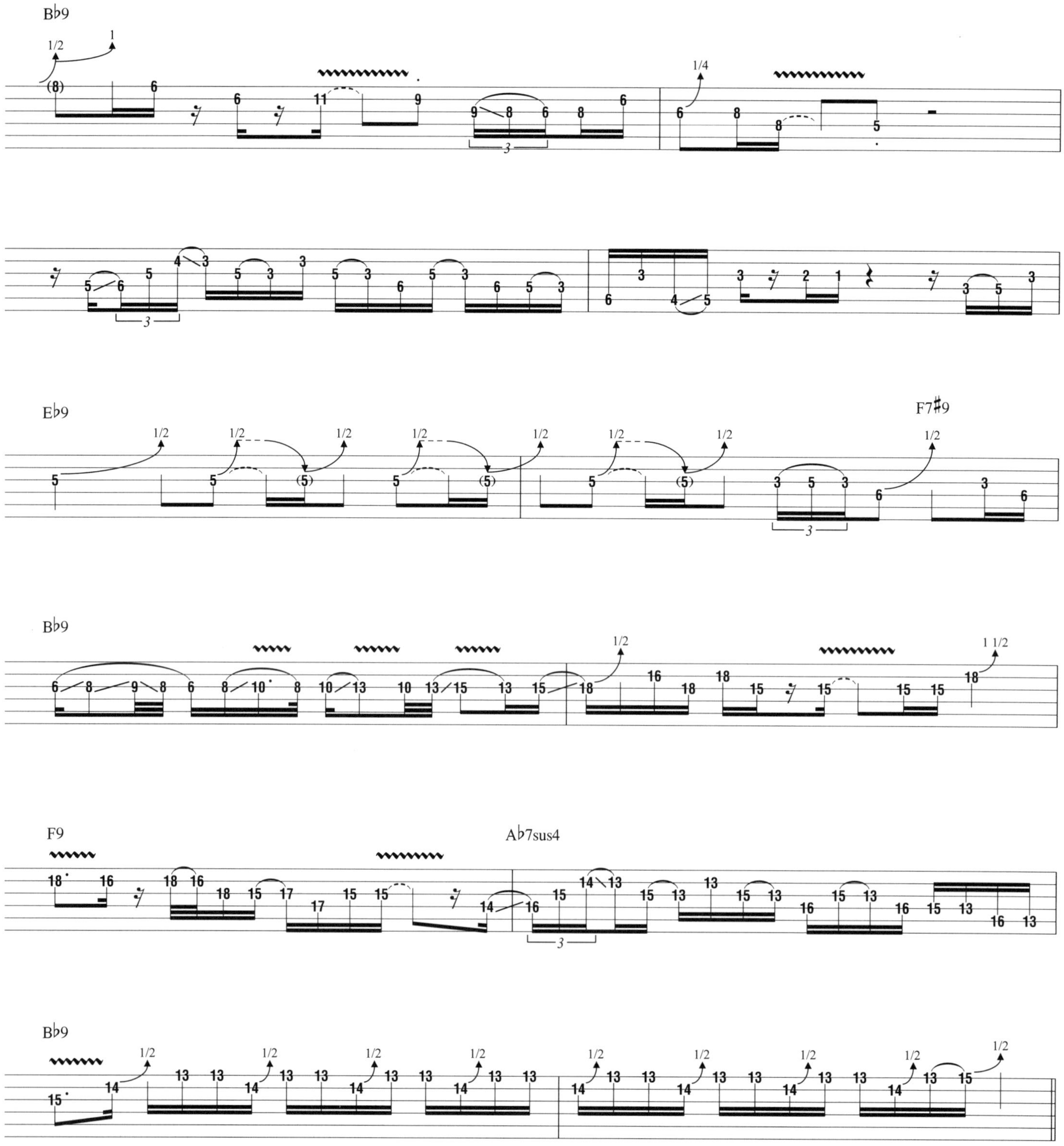
B♭9
E♭9
F7♯9
B♭9
F9
A♭7sus4
B♭9

Example 32: Minor blues jam

Key of B♭m

(3:13)

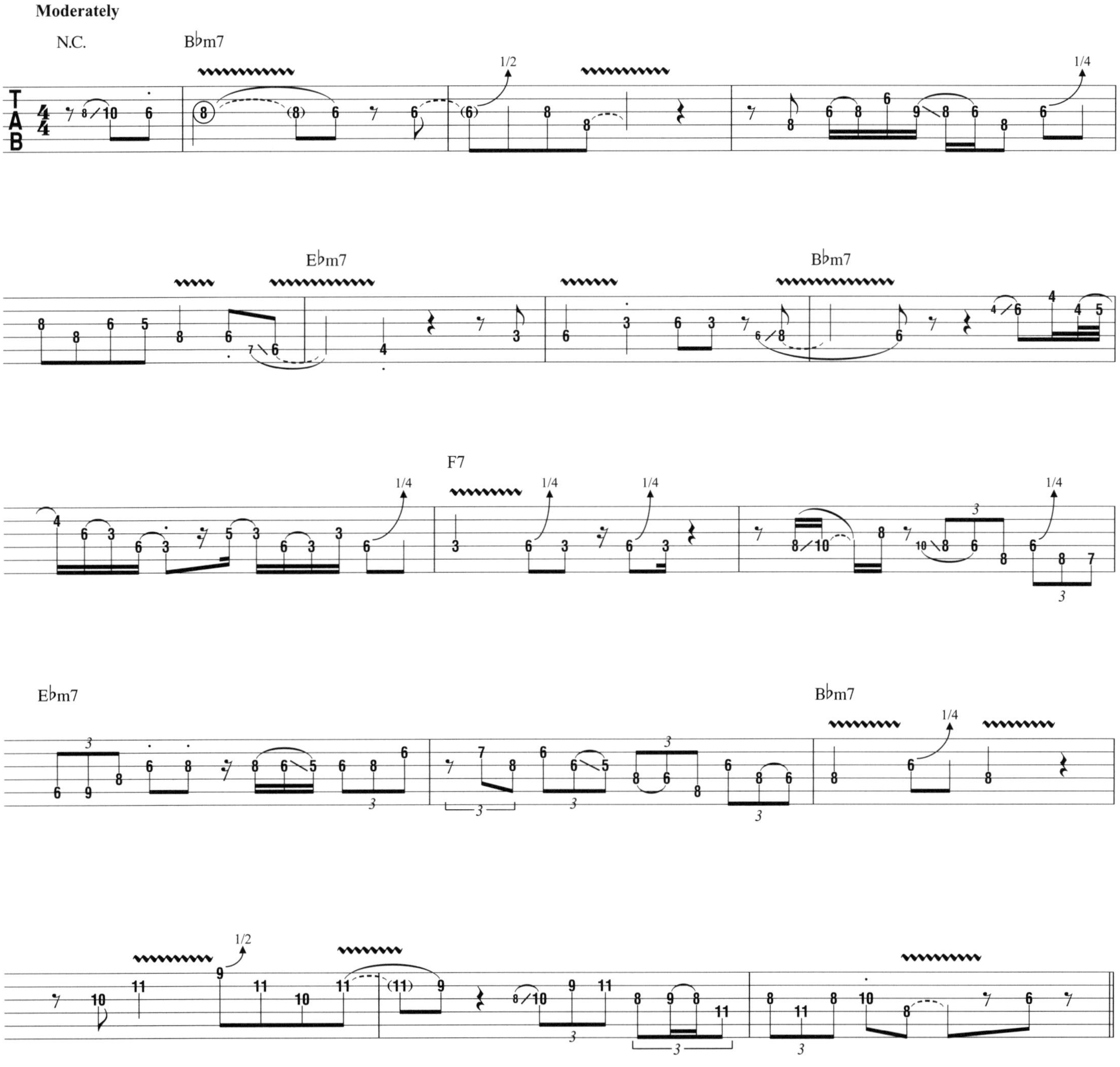

B♭m7
let ring
let ring
let ring
w/ fingers
E♭m7
B♭m7
F7
E♭m7
B♭m7
w/ fingers
w/ fingers
B♭m7

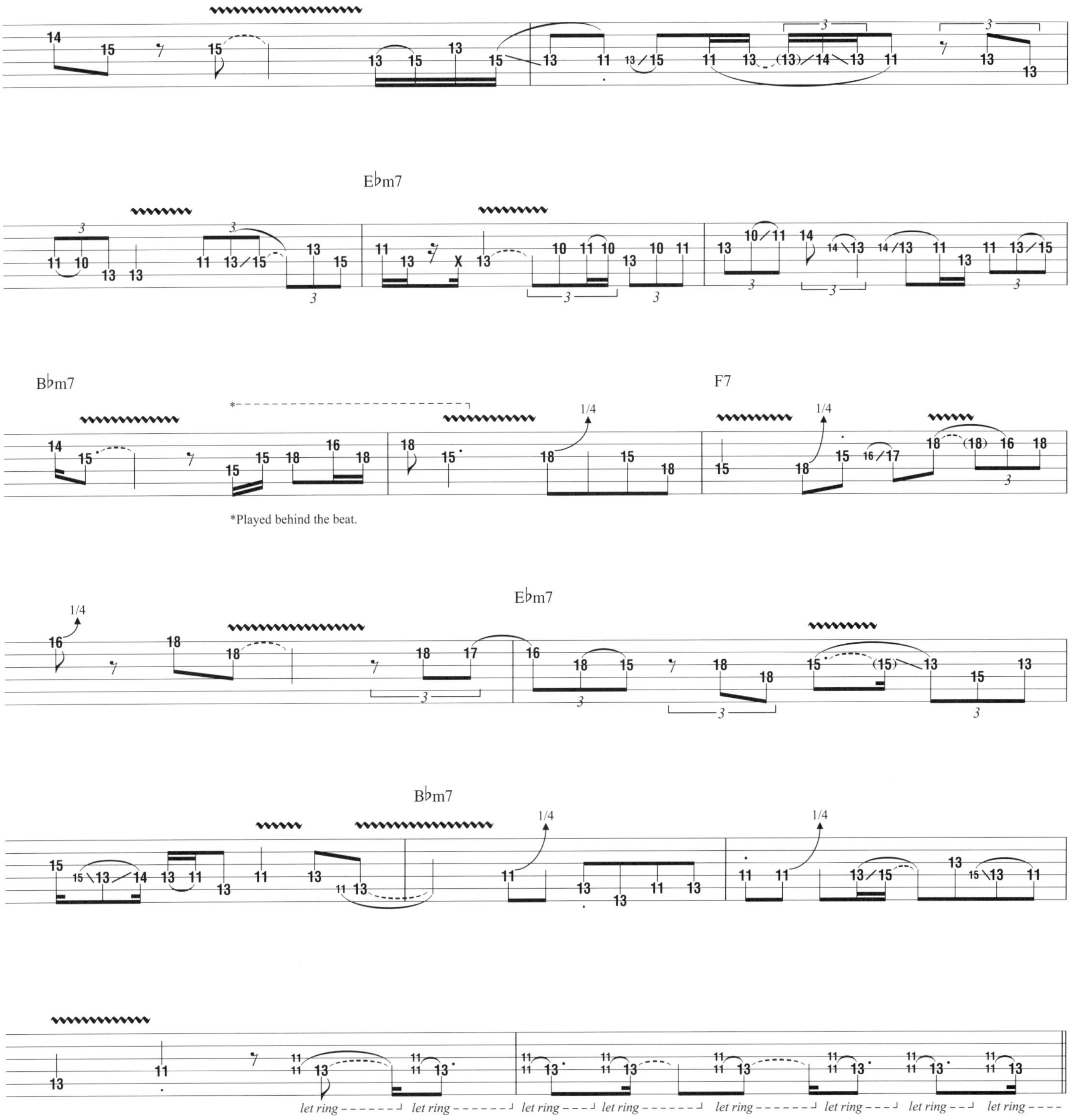
E♭m7
B♭m7
F7
*Played behind the beat.
E♭m7
B♭m7
let ring

Example 33: Mixolydian licks
Key of A
(6:04)

Fast $(\sqcap = \overline{}^3\overline{})$

N.C.(A7)

Example 34: Minor 2nd and major 7th as passing tones
Key of A
(6:49)

Fast

N.C.(A5)

*T=Thumb on 6th string.

Example 35: Jam

Key of B♭m

(10:30)

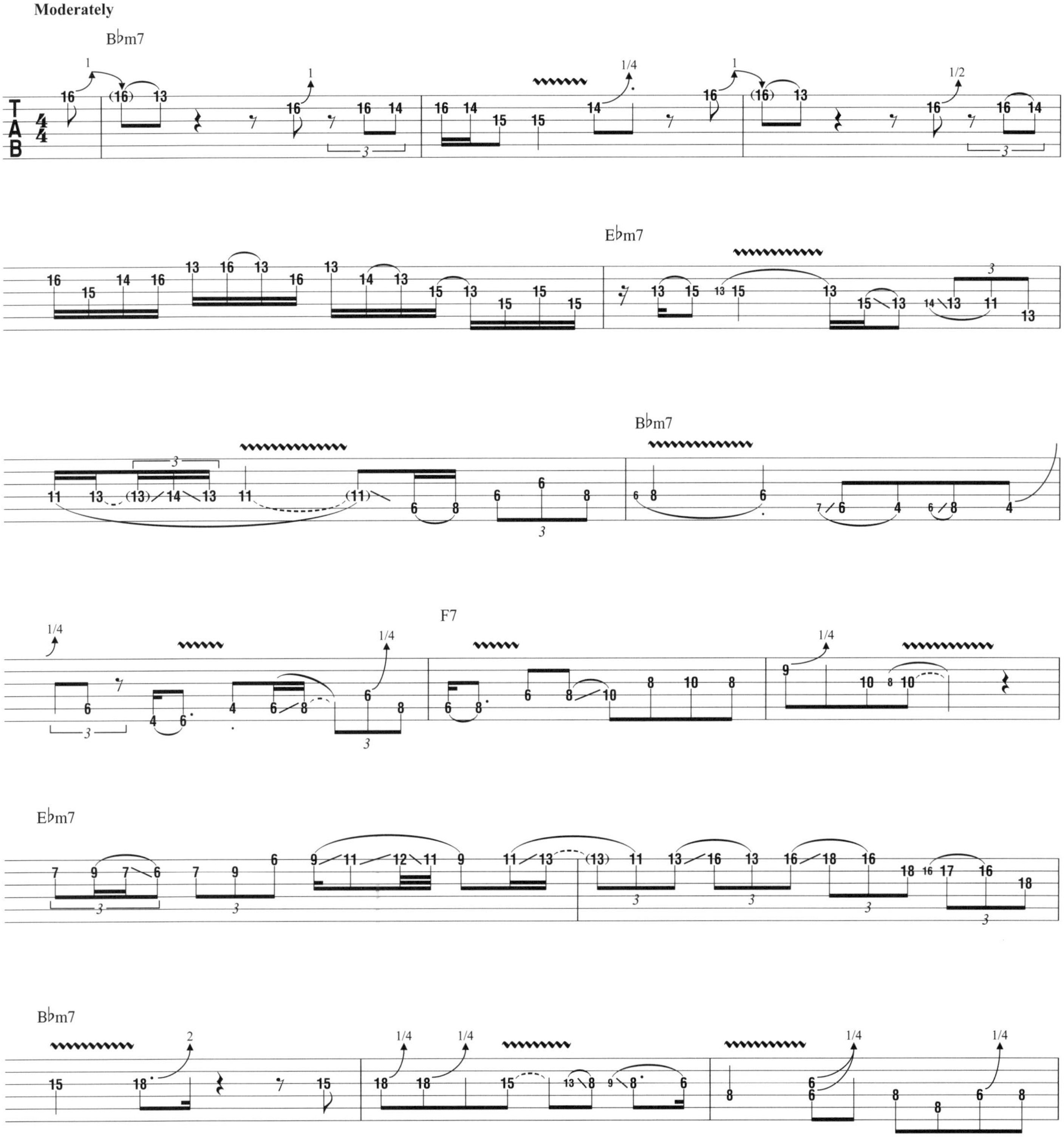

B♭m7
E♭m7
w/ fingers
let ring
B♭m7
let ring
F7
E♭m7
w/ pick
B♭m7
let ring
B♭m7

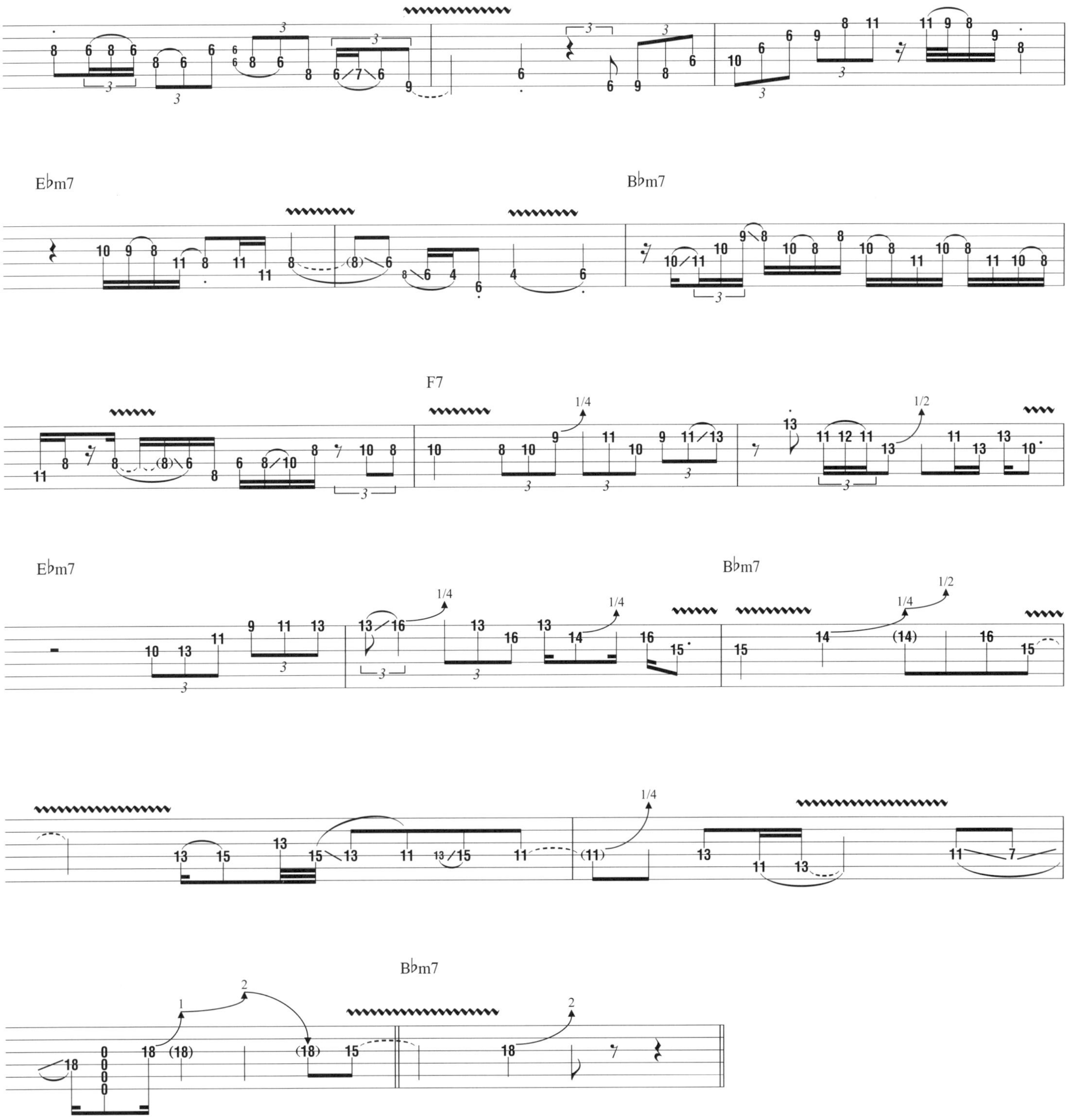
E♭m7
B♭m7
F7
E♭m7
B♭m7
B♭m7

The Blues in Your Playing

Example 36: Major-minor 3rd rub
Key of A
(1:15)

Example 37: Using the ♭5th
Key of A
(2:36)

Example 38: Over-bends à la Albert King and Buddy Guy
Key of A
(3:59)

Example 39: Odd finger bends
Key of A
(4:11)

Freely

Example 40: Combination bend and slide
Key of A
(4:31)

Freely

*T=Thumb on
6th string.

Example 41: Connecting fretboard positions

Key of A

(5:23)

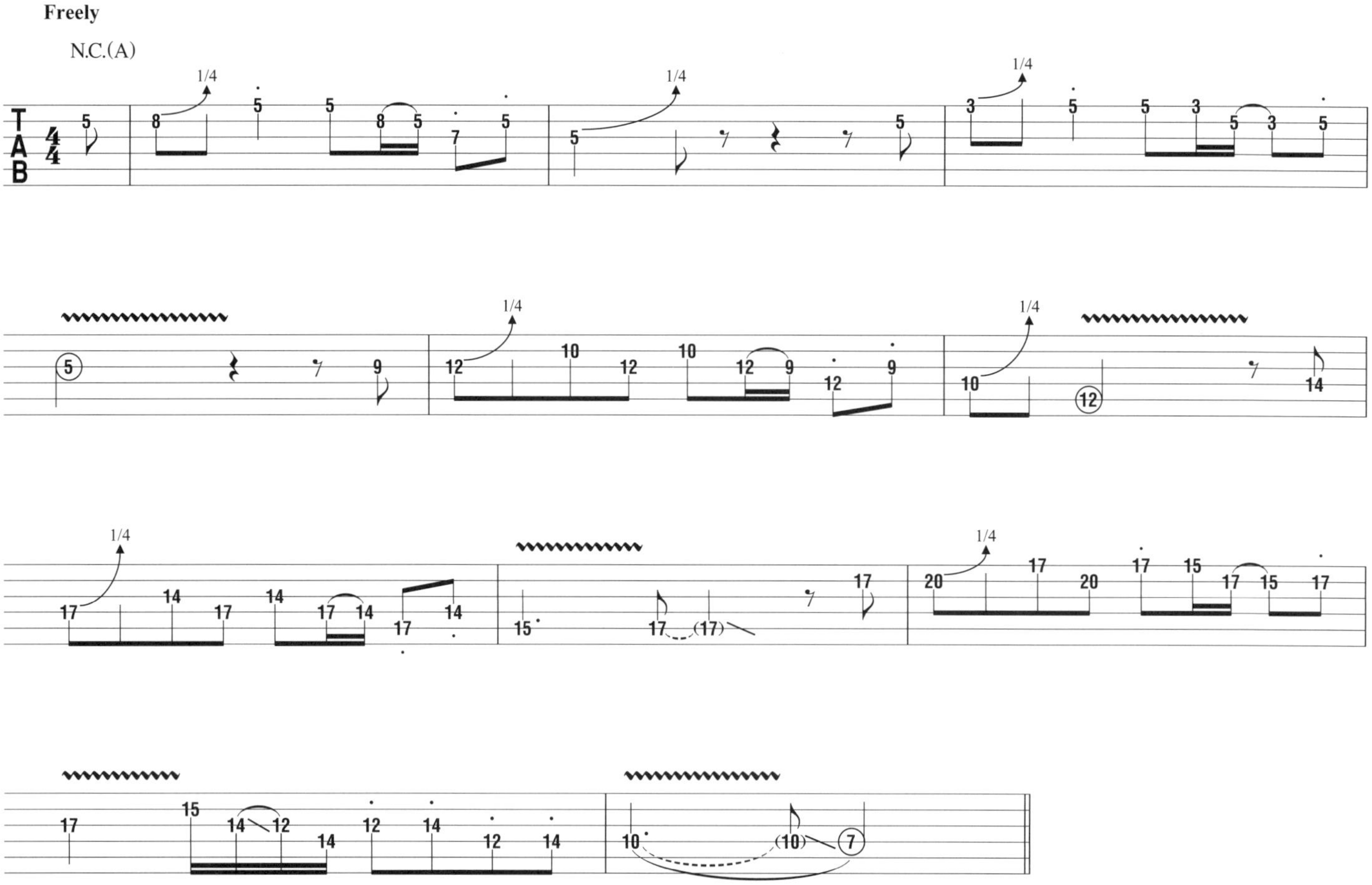

Example 42: One lick in several octaves

Key of A

(6:02)

*T=Thumb on 6th string.

Example 43: Outro jam

Key of A

(6:22)

Moderately fast (♫ = ♩♪)

*T=Thumb on 6th string.

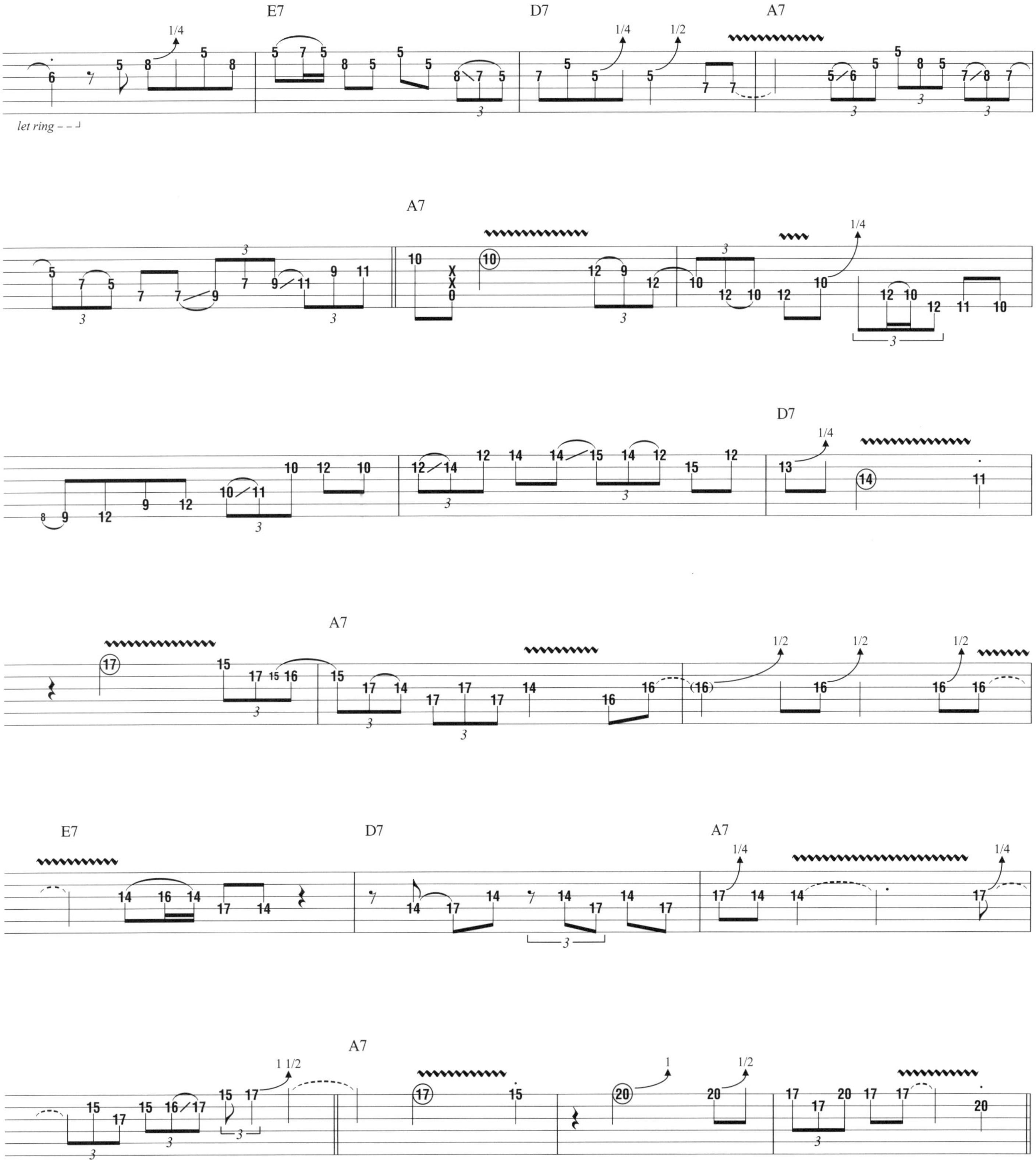
E7
D7
A7
let ring
A7
D7
A7
E7
D7
A7
A7

RHYTHM TAB LEGEND

Rhythm Tab is a form of notation that adds rhythmic values to the traditional tab staff.

TABLATURE graphically represents the guitar fingerboard. Each horizontal line represents a string, and each number represents a fret. Rhythmic values are shown using ovals, stems, and dots.

4th string, 2nd fret, played as a whole note

1st & 2nd strings open, played together as a half note

An open G chord, played as a quarter note and eighth notes

An open D chord, played and held for 3½ beats

Definitions for Special Guitar Notation

HALF-STEP BEND: Strike the note and bend up 1/2 step.

WHOLE-STEP BEND: Strike the note and bend up one step.

SLIGHT (MICROTONE) BEND: Strike the note and bend up 1/4 step.

BEND AND RELEASE: Strike the note and bend up as indicated, then release back to the original note. Only the first note is struck.

PRE-BEND: Bend the note as indicated, then strike it.

GRACE NOTE PRE-BEND AND RELEASE: Bend the note as indicated. Strike it and release the bend back to the original note.

UNISON BEND: Strike the two notes simultaneously and bend the lower note up to the pitch of the higher.

HOLD BEND: While sustaining bent note, strike note on different string.

VIBRATO: The string is vibrated by rapidly bending and releasing the note with the fretting hand.

WIDE VIBRATO: The pitch is varied to a greater degree by vibrating with the fretting hand.

HAMMER-ON: Strike the first (lower) note with one finger, then sound the higher note (on the same string) with another finger by fretting it without picking.

PULL-OFF: Place both fingers on the notes to be sounded. Strike the first note and without picking, pull the finger off to sound the second (lower) note.

HAMMER FROM NOWHERE: Sound note(s) by hammering with fret hand finger only.

GRACE NOTE SLUR: Strike the note and immediately hammer-on (or pull-off) as indicated.

GRACE NOTE SLUR (CLUSTER): Strike the notes and immediately hammer-on (or pull-off) as indicated.

LEGATO SLIDE: Strike the first note and then slide the same fret-hand finger up or down to the second note. The second note is not struck.

SHIFT SLIDE: Same as legato slide, except the second note is struck.

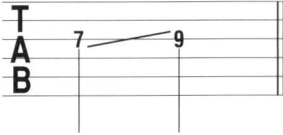

GRACE NOTE SLIDE: Quickly slide into the note from below or above.

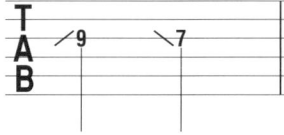

TRILL: Very rapidly alternate between the notes indicated by continuously hammering on and pulling off.

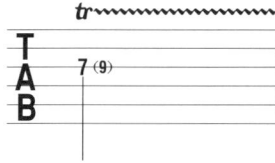

TAPPING: Hammer ("tap") the fret indicated with the pick-hand index or middle finger and pull off to the note fretted by the fret hand.

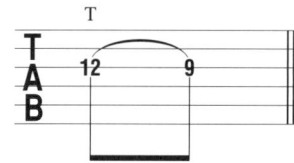

NATURAL HARMONIC: Strike the note while the fret-hand lightly touches the string directly over the fret indicated.

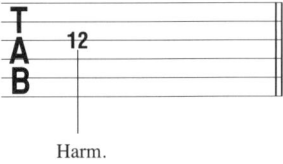

PINCH HARMONIC: The note is fretted normally and a harmonic is produced by adding the edge of the thumb or the tip of the index finger of the pick hand to the normal pick attack.

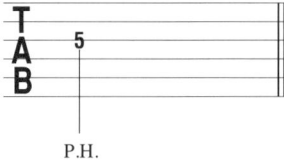

HARP HARMONIC: The note is fretted normally and a harmonic is produced by gently resting the pick hand's index finger directly above the indicated fret (in parentheses) while the pick hand's thumb or pick assists by plucking the appropriate string.

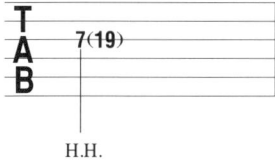

PICK SCRAPE: The edge of the pick is rubbed down (or up) the string, producing a scratchy sound.

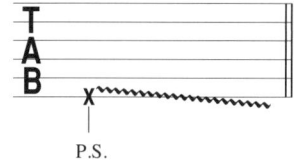

MUFFLED STRINGS: A percussive sound is produced by laying the fret hand across the string(s) without depressing, and striking them with the pick hand.

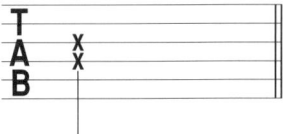

PALM MUTING: The note is partially muted by the pick hand lightly touching the string(s) just before the bridge.

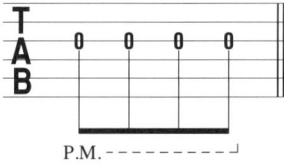

RAKE: Drag the pick across the strings indicated with a single motion.

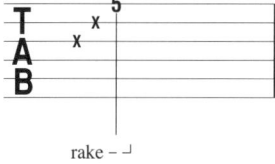

TREMOLO PICKING: The note is picked as rapidly and continuously as possible.

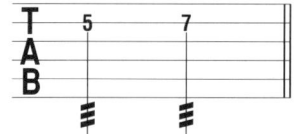

ARPEGGIATE: Play the notes of the chord indicated by quickly rolling them from bottom to top.

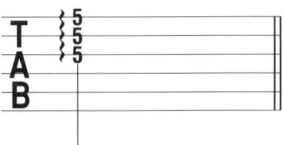

VIBRATO BAR DIVE AND RETURN: The pitch of the note or chord is dropped a specified number of steps (in rhythm), then returned to the original pitch.

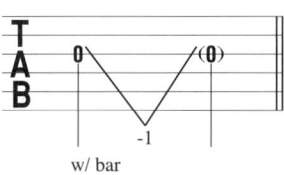

VIBRATO BAR SCOOP: Depress the bar just before striking the note, then quickly release the bar.

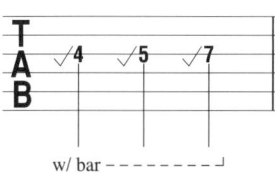

VIBRATO BAR DIP: Strike the note and then immediately drop a specified number of steps, then release back to the original pitch.

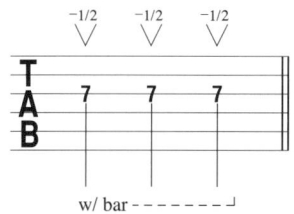

Additional Musical Definitions

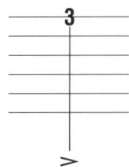

(accent) • Accentuate note (play it louder)

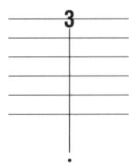

(staccato) • Play the note short

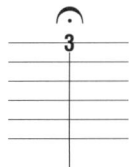

(fermata) • A hold or pause

• Downstroke

• Upstroke

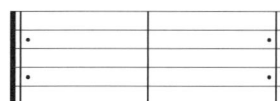

• Repeat measures between signs

NOTE: Tablature numbers in parentheses are used when:
- The note is sustained, but a new articulation begins (such as a hammer-on, pull-off, slide, or bend), or
- A bend is released.
- A note sustains while crossing from one staff to another.

HOT LICKS

For the first time, the legendary Hot Licks guitar instruction video series is being made available in book format with online access to the classic video footage. All of the guitar tab from the original video booklets has been re-transcribed and edited using modern-day technology to provide you with the most accurate transcriptions ever created for this series. Plus, we've included tab for examples that were previously not transcribed, providing you with the most comprehensive Hot Licks guitar lessons yet. Each book with online video is available for $19.99 each.

HAL•LEONARD®
Prices, contents, and availability subject to change without notice.